NCEA PAPERS

THE CONSTITUTION, GOVERNMENTAL AID AND CATHOLIC HIGHER EDUCATION

By Rev. Robert F. Drinan, S.J.

National Catholic Educational Association
NCEA Papers, Box 667, Dayton, Ohio 45401

ABOUT THE AUTHOR

Father Robert F. Drinan, S.J., is Dean of the Boston College Law School and Professor of Family Law and Church-State Relations. He holds B.A. and M.A. degrees from Boston College, the LL.B. and LL.M. from the Georgetown University Law Center, and the S.T.L. from the Gregorian University. A member of the Bar of Massachusetts, the District of Columbia and the United States Supreme Court, he is chairman of the Massachusetts Bar Association's Committees on the Administration of Justice and Family Law and Chairman-Elect of the Family Law Section of the American Bar Association. He is the author of *Religion, the Courts and Public Policy* (McGraw-Hill, 1963) and has contributed articles to a number of other books and journals. He belongs to many civic organizations and is Chairman of the Massachusetts Advisory Committee to the U. S. Commission on Civil Rights.

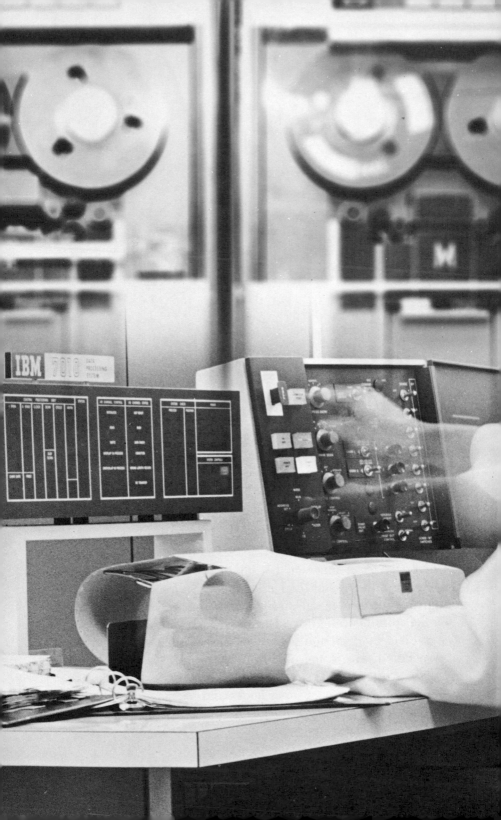

An unarticulated feeling of pessimism seems to characterize the mood of officials and educators presently associated with Catholic higher education. This pessimism is also present—but perhaps to a lesser extent—among all educators at private colleges. A mood of uneasiness about the future is especially prevalent at small, private, liberal arts colleges which are located at a substantial distance from a metropolitan area.

The ultimate source of the uneasiness at non-Catholic colleges centers on one thing: money. At Catholic colleges and universities the anxiety over money is made infinitely more profound by the nagging question: are Catholic colleges still necessary?

The misgivings of those involved in Catholic higher education are further deepened by the very complexity and indefinability of the term "Catholic higher education." The unplanned and unorganized state of "Catholic higher education" as revealed in the Danforth study, *Church-Sponsored*

Higher Education in the United States (American Council on Education, 1966) has led to a widespread desire among everyone connected with "Catholic higher education" for an agency with almost the powers of a czar which could bring it about that the academic mediocrity (or worse) present in so many Catholic colleges might no longer embarrass those associated with those Catholic colleges which have a chance of being at least close to top-rated institutions.

The mood about the future of Catholic colleges is further complicated by the fact that most major Catholic colleges cannot in any realistic sense be described as colleges controlled by the religious groups which founded them. The religious order may, however, still "operate" the college even though academic (but seldom fiscal) control has passed or should pass to the lay faculty.

It seems accurate, moreover, to state that the present—and prospective—faculty members at Catholic colleges are not confident that the religious orders will be far-sighted in the actions they take (or refuse to take) in expanding the base of support, direction and government of Catholic colleges.

Despite the complexity and the unpredictability of what might happen to Catholic colleges in the next generation these institutions share with all private colleges one primal urge and instinct: the need to survive. The actual survival of the private college in America is a matter of conjecture. There is evidence to support the prediction that the private college is in the process of being phased out just as the private academy of the last century gradually became extinct as public high schools became compulsory.

In order to try to analyze and comprehend the multiple forces operating on the private and church-related college in America the following topics will be explored:

I. The history and role of the private and church-related college in America.

II. Recent federal and state legislation giving assistance to private colleges.

III. The Church-State problems in programs of governmental aid, with particular reference to the judicial decisions in the case of the four church-related colleges in Maryland.

IV. The options and strategies available to church-related colleges with regard to governmental aid for secular academic purposes.

I. THE ROLE OF THE PRIVATE, CHURCH-RELATED COLLEGE IN AMERICAN HISTORY

The amazing identification of Protestantism and Americanism in the whole history of the United States was both the cause and the result of the Protestant-affiliated colleges attended until the recent past by most of the nation's leaders. The secularization of so many of these colleges has had an enormous impact on the outlook of the younger graduates of these schools now in public life. But the accumulated pride and prestige of these once Protestant institutions is so intense that alumni loyalty to these universities constitutes the backbone of a deeply felt and heavily financed national "crusade" to save the "private" college.

The virtues of the "private" college, however, are not self-revealing. Yet the literature of national "give-to-the-college-of-your-choice" campaigns and the brochures of the development offices of private universities seem to assume that the desirability of maintaining strong "private" colleges is self-evident.

The term "private", however, does not even suggest the orientation or the value system which a "private" college seeks to communicate. Often the term "liberal arts college" is added to the term "private", but the term "liberal arts" furnishes even less of an identification than the concept of "private" because public universities can assuredly excel just as much in teaching the liberal arts as can private colleges.

There is therefore a rather compelling need to clarify the exact purposes of the "crusade" to save the "private" college. It is not enough, moreover, simply to state that the nation needs diversity and pluralism in higher education, unless it can also be demonstrated that these qualities cannot be furnished by public universities.

If the survival of private colleges is desirable, furthermore, it does not suffice to assert merely that they are "partners" with public universities; they must have some unique virtues in and of themselves. In short they must have some values to communicate which it is impossible (or at least very difficult) for public universities to transmit.

It would seem that the uniqueness of a private college inheres in its approach to the liberal arts or the humanities since a college's approach to the physical and social sciences would seem to be substantially the same everywhere. Yet in the very area of the humanities the claims of the private colleges remain ambiguous. Professor Robert S. Morison, commenting on this phenomenon in his perceptive essay in *The Contemporary University: U.S.A.* (Beacon Press, 1966), noted that "there now seems to be a certain vagueness . . . in the minds of the humanists themselves . . . as to why it is worthwhile to study culture." (p. 103). The vagueness of the humanists' claims may come, Professor Morison thinks, from a "basic lack of self-confidence" or from the humanists' "very real difficulty in being sure that they really do have something important to say about some of the more spectacular contemporary moral questions deriving from the use of atomic energy, the uncontrolled growth of populations, or the possibility of directing human evolution." (p. 104) Professor Morison also suggests that the vagueness of the humanists is probably attributable in part to the "ambiguous position of morals in a modern university." For a variety of reasons universities have adopted a "largely custodial and analytical attitude toward problems of value" (p. 105)—an attitude which inhibits advocates of the humanities at private colleges from asserting any very clear or specific objectives which they can accomplish in whole or in part more fruitfully than a public university.

The dramatic if not the drastic decline in the proportionate enrollment of students at private colleges may well be attributable to the inherent ambiguity of the claims of the defenders of the private college. On the other hand it may be that the forces in American life which brought about the apotheosis of the public elementary and secondary school have become so overwhelming that the private college is living on borrowed time.

The decline of the private college was perhaps unconsciously commenced by the federal government in the Land-Grant Act of 1862 by which vast tracts of land were given to the states for the establishment of colleges which would specialize in agriculture and the practical arts. By this one grant of massive funds to public colleges the United States government radically changed the dominant orientation of higher education in America from the humanities and the liberal arts to the pragmatic and utilitarian application of the practical sciences.

There is no record that the private colleges in 1862 protested the Land-Grant Act or that they saw in this federal law the adoption of a public policy which would inevitably change the meaning and mission of higher education in America.

It is intriguing and significant to note that, despite the fabulous actual and potential wealth of the land-grant or state universities, private and church-related colleges have been established and extended during the last century in a way totally unprecedented in the history of Western civilization. No nation, no continent, no century has ever witnessed the growth of some 2,000 colleges and universities, 870 of which in 1963 were still church-related.

It seems difficult to believe that the vision, the energy and the determination which went into the establishment of these non-public colleges and universities is now so dissipated that these institutions will either decline into mediocrity or become at least quasi-state universities. But such indeed appears to be their reliably predicted future—unless, that is, a revolution in thinking occurs within the near future.

Catholic colleges have in general remained the most value-oriented of all the church-related and private colleges in America. Such a status brings potential advantages and definite disadvantages. The potential advantages arise from the real diversity and true pluralism which Catholic colleges represent in American higher education. The disadvantages come from the possibility that Catholic colleges might be considered to be so denominational and sectarian that they would be deemed legally disqualified from receiving governmental assistance. Whether the advantages or the disadvantages will be superior depends on what public policy and constitutional law America in the next few years will adopt, and on what Catholic higher education will become within the next generation.

Let us then review recent federal and state legislation designed to aid higher education. Such a review will be undertaken in order to discover the principles and policies affecting higher education with which American society is wrestling.

II. RECENT FEDERAL AND STATE LEGISLATION ON HIGHER EDUCATION

Reflecting the pragmatism and utilitarianism which is so much a part of the educational philosophy of America, the Congress of the United States has almost invariably given financial assistance to higher education only for specific scientific, military or practical purposes. With the possible exception of the G.I. Bill of Rights, the federal government has concentrated on categorical assistance for colleges; the National Science Foundation, the programs to help medical and nursing students and the National Defense Education Act of 1958 are familiar examples of the pragmatic (indeed sometimes the "panic") approach which Congress has taken with regard to the needs of higher education.

The precedent-shattering Higher Education Act of 1963 followed this same approach but its basic purposes have now been expanded. But the National Humanities Foundation, finally established in 1965, may possibly constitute a dramatic reversal of steadfast congressional adherence to a utilitarian policy of giving aid only when confronted with a crisis in higher education.

Congress has presumably committed the federal government irreversibly to the financing of higher education. But it is well to remember that in 1963, during the long Senate debate on the nation's first Higher Education Facilities Act, a total of 26 senators, or over one-fourth of the Senate, voted to exclude *all* church-related colleges from any participation in federal aid to higher education.

Even if, however, federal appropriations for all colleges increase dramatically, no foreseeable annual federal subsidy can really solve the principal problem of the private college, the problem of the annual deficit resulting merely from mounting operating costs. If, for example, in 1970 the federal government appropriated five billion dollars (or about twice its commitment in 1967) for the 8,000,000 students expected to be in college in 1970, the total sum available to colleges would be only $625 per student—or less than 50 percent of the loss sustained by a good college for every person enrolled.

Even to think of federal aid in terms of income per student is, of course, misleading since federal subsidies are given for research, for construction costs, for student loans and other specific objectives unrelated to the over-all operating costs of colleges. One must face the fact, furthermore, that federal aid for instructional salaries, the greatest single expense in every college budget, is not now foreseeably predictable.

Many proposals for increased federal aid to higher education continue to be advanced; tax deductions of tuition for parents, long-term tax savings for students who borrow their tuition, and other imaginative devices would certainly help private colleges. But the stark reality remains: private colleges cannot continue to excel when the education they impart costs at least twice as much as the tuition they charge and when public universities enjoy massive and mounting governmental subsidies.

An understanding of the crisis of the nation's private colleges has been growing at the federal level but the failure of the states to act deserves exploration.

STATE PLANS FOR PRIVATE COLLEGES

The absence until the very recent past of substantial programs of federal assistance for private colleges has not prompted the vast majority of states to initiate their own programs of aid for non-public colleges and universities. With the exception of state programs in New York, California, Wisconsin and a few other places, most states have expended their available funds on the strengthening and expansion of public institutions of higher education. Reasons leading to this pattern include the powerful national thrust towards furnishing a *free* college education to all, the restrictions in state constitutions against aid to church-affiliated schools and the almost total lack of any organization to speak for the private colleges of any state.

Perhaps the most fundamental reason for the paucity of state programs to give financial assistance to private colleges is the lack of realization on the part of society—and, to a large extent, on the part of educators in private colleges—of the hazardous and worsening fiscal condition of the private college. College officials and trustees are understandably reluctant to reveal their poverty to prospective professors and students. If the given facts about the bleak future of poorly endowed private colleges are ever disclosed it is done in monographs read only by experts on the financing of higher education.

But the fact is undeniable that virtually every private college will inevitably be inferior to state-financed institutions unless there is discovered for the private college *some* source of financing comparable to that available annually to the state unversity. The massive infusion of millions of dollars into private higher education for faculty salaries by the Ford Foundation several years ago was probably the most dramatic demonstration up to now of the coming crisis of private colleges. The Ford grants signalized the emergence of annual substantial contributions from industry to non-public higher education. But even the wealth of the foundations and of major corporations cannot be expected to match the affluence of a state which is determined to commit its taxing power to the ideal of maximizing equal opportunity in higher education for all young adults.

The crucial problem confronting private colleges which has not been faced up to by either the federal or the state governments is the need for substantial financing for basic operating costs of the university. The state university has a built-in annual guarantee of appropriations adequate for its operations; special new laws for improvement and expansion of facilities must be fought for. But even if private colleges could receive under federal and state programs periodic allotments sufficient for normal improvement and expansion of facilities (a situation which is clearly not yet realizable by the private college), the critical problem of the annual and mounting deficit by reason of operating expenses would not be even partially resolved.

Federal and state programs to aid private colleges, therefore, however commendable they may be, yield no assurance that they can save the private college from extinction. Indeed most programs designed to assist private colleges merely increase the facilities of these institutions and thereby escalate their deficits!

III. CHURCH-STATE PROBLEMS IN GOVERNMENTAL AID TO CHURCH-RELATED COLLEGES

On October 15, 1966, the United States Supreme Court refused to review the first judicial decision in American jurisprudence which denied aid to church-related colleges on the ground that such aid violated the establishment clause of the federal Constitution. This decision of Maryland's highest court deserves a thorough analysis but first some

general background material on state aid to church-connected institutions must be reviewed.

There is a widespread but amorphous feeling in American public opinion that *all* aid to religiously affiliated institutions is unconstitutional. The most tangible "fall-out" from Supreme Court opinions over the last 20 years has been the commonly held assumption that the no-establishment prohibition of the First Amendment has erected a wall of separation between Church and State, a wall which means *"no-aid-to-religion."*

It may be that vast numbers of Americans have exaggerated the "no-aid-to-religion" doctrine of the Supreme Court because such a doctrine confirms their most fundamental convictions or prejudices about the inadvisability of giving public support to parochial schools. The fact is, however, that the "no-aid-to-religion" principle endorsed by the Supreme Court is by no means as categorical or definitive as those who employ it so often imply.

It is astonishing that the Supreme Court has spoken only once in all of American history with regard to the effect of the First Amendment on financial support to church-related schools. This one occasion was, of course, the 1947 *Everson* decision where the Supreme Court, in a 5 to 4 split, permitted New Jersey to use public funds to transport children to a church-related school. During the last 20 years the Supreme Court has refused to give any further rulings on the constitutionality of governmental assistance to church-related educational institutions. The court has moreover added confusion to an already complex question by allowing inconsistent decisions by various state courts to remain unreviewed by the nation's highest tribunal. A judgment by the Supreme Court of Connecticut, sustaining bus ride legislation benefiting private school children was, for example, refused review by the U. S. Supreme Court as were other decisions which reached opposite results in the states.

It should be clear, therefore, that, despite all the sound and fury of proponents and opponents of federal aid to church-related schools, there is very little law at the federal level with respect to this problem. To be sure, the Supreme Court in its decisions sustaining Sunday laws and its rulings against devotional exercises in public schools reaffirmed its ban on aid to religion. But this principle cannot resolve the question of the constitutionality of aid given for secular purposes to be carried out by a church-related institution.

The crucial principles of the *Everson* decision consequently must be fully understood. These principles, which constitute the only real federal constitutional law that exists on the question of state aid to sectarian schools, can be stated as follows:

(1) No state money may be intentionally or purposefully given to religion or irreligion.

(2) In the distribution of the benefits of "public welfare legislation" no one may be benefited or disadvantaged because of his religious faith or lack of it.

Applying these principles, the majority of the court in *Everson* found that the state was not giving *purposeful* aid to religion in financing bus transportation for pupils attending denominational schools. The court found that a benefit of this nature was a result of "public welfare legislation" and consequently could not be withheld from citizens simply because of their religious faith.

The minority of the court, in vigorous dissents, concluded that the Catholic schools attended by the pupils in question were undeniably benefited by the funds received by the children for school bus transportation and that therefore the New Jersey statute must be declared unconstitutional because it resulted in giving aid to religion.

It must be confessed that neither the majority nor the minority opinions in *Everson* are very clear or satisfactory. Their inherent ambiguity increases as the complexity of the issues involved in judging the secular-sectarian character of a church-affiliated school emerges. One could indeed argue persuasively that the Supreme Court has a duty to review a case in this area and to give to legislators and judges some better guidelines than the uneasy 5-4 decision in *Everson* has furnished.

The only Supreme Court decision besides *Everson* which really furnishes any principles for the application of the "no-aid-to-religion" doctrine is the court's ruling in 1961 sustaining the constitutionality of Sunday laws. A new element or at least a new emphasis was added by the court to the test set forth in *Everson*. The Supreme Court held in the Sunday law cases that legislation could be constitutional if neither its primary purpose or effect was to aid religion. Sunday-closing laws, the court found, were designed in their present form to provide a uniform day of rest for all citizens. If some incidental benefit to religion resulted from the selection of Sunday as the common day of rest such aid is not proscribed by the no-establishment clause since neither the purpose nor the primary effect of Sunday laws is to aid religion.

The Supreme Court, however, in the Sunday law cases, went beyond this requirement of neutrality in purpose and effect and stated that the government, in carrying out its secular goals, must, if at all possible, avoid infringing on the religious freedom of *all* citizens. Chief Justice Warren put it this way:

"If the state regulates conduct by enacting a general law within its power, the purpose and effect of which is to advance the state's secular goals, the statute is valid *despite its indirect burden on religious observance unless a state may accomplish its purpose by means which do not impose such a burden.*" (emphasis supplied)

This principle is, of course, applicable not only to the Sabbath observers or Sabbatarians who litigated the Sunday laws but also to those who claim that the state places at least an "indirect burden" on their "religious observance" when the state advances its secular goals in education by utilizing exclusively public and non-denominational instrumentalities.

A principle with even more implications than the rationale of the Sunday law decisions was enunciated by the Supreme

Court in an opinion handed down on the same day in June, 1963 as the ruling banning the reading of the Bible from the public school. In this little known opinion the Supreme Court held that the state of South Carolina could not refuse unemployment compensation to Mrs. Adele Sherbert, a Seventh Day Adventist, who could not, for reasons of conscience, work on Saturday. In a mandate which broadened the *Everson* principle forbidding discrimination on the basis of religious faith, the Supreme Court stated in effect that no disabilities may be placed on citizens because they happen to hold religious convictions different from those of the majority. Ironically, the long-term thrust of the relatively unknown *Sherbert* decision may be more important than the effect of the celebrated decisions eliminating the reading of the Bible and the recitation of prayers from the public school.

It is not possible to draw from these few decisions of the Supreme Court any consistent pattern on which to base a prediction as to what the court will do when eventually it must decide the constitutionality of tax support for secular educational objectives carried out under the auspices of a church-affiliated institution. The one thing which is clear is that any program whose intention or *primary* effect is to aid religion will be struck down. But when a state has no intention of aiding or inhibiting religion and where a "non-primary" effect is the advancement or inhibition of religion, the program will not offend the establishment clause or the "no-aid-to-religion" principle.

The Supreme Court therefore has *not* stated that all aid to a sectarian institution is unconstitutional. Nor has the court even approached the question of determining the point at which tax-supported legitimate secular objectives carried out by a church-related body might begin to have the "primary effect" of aiding religion. Nor has the court furnished very much guidance as to appropriate priorities between the demands of the free exercise of religion guarantee of the First Amendment and the no-establishment clause of the same amendment.

In view of the very undeveloped state of Supreme Court rulings on the question of aid to church-related schools it is anomalous if not amazing that the highest court of Maryland, in a 4 to 3 ruling, declared that state grants to three church-related colleges for the construction of dormitories and science buildings were in violation not of the Maryland Constitution (which is silent on the point) but of the First Amendment to the federal Constitution!

THE MARYLAND COLLEGES DECISION

In 1784 Maryland initiated a plan to aid private colleges. Doubts about the constitutionality of this program were resolved by Maryland's Court of Appeals in 1954 in its unanimous decision validating a grant of $1,500,000 to Johns Hopkins University for the construction of an engineering building. The issue in this lawsuit, however, was not a Church-State dispute but one over the legality of Maryland pledging its credit on behalf of a non-public agency.

The Maryland plan to assist private colleges never involved any very systematic scheme to give substantial financing to the private colleges attended by a very significant number of Maryland's young adults. The plan involved only periodic matching grants by the state legislature to private colleges on a rotating basis. The grants invalidated in 1966 in the case initiated by the Horace Mann League included an authorization on a matching basis for a science wing and dining hall at Western Maryland College, a Methodist institution, an identical sum for Hood College, a unit related to the United Church, for a dormitory and classroom building, and two sums of $750,000 each for the construction of science buildings at St. Joseph's College and the College of Notre Dame, both Catholic institutions.

The Horace Mann League, a Maryland-based non-profit corporation organized "for the purpose of fostering and strengthening the American public school system," based its attack on the constitutionality of the four grants in issue not on a contention that no church-related college can legally

receive tax support but on the proposition that such aid is barred only if the connection between the school and its sponsoring church is "substantial" or "intense." The plaintiffs moreover did not openly allege that a college with a close connection with a church will subvert or even change the secular learning it communicates by permeating it with sectarian values. The plaintiffs seemed rather to assume that tax support, though given for stated secular purposes, will nonetheless aid religion because it will liberate other funds which, but for the tax support, the church sponsoring a college would have to expend on the dissemination of secular knowledge.

The crucial question therefore is the nature, extent and intensity of the "relatedness" by which a college is joined to a church. Prior to the Maryland decision the law and educators had tended to assume that all institutions chartered by a state to grant academic degrees and accredited as liberal arts colleges should be classified as institutions of higher education eligible to receive all available benefits regardless of the sectarian or non-sectarian character of the ultimate governing board of any particular institution. Such an approach was clearly the cornerstone of the Federal Higher Education Facilities Act of 1963, although it should not be forgotten that opposition to the inclusion of church-related colleges in that bill was expressed by several influential public school organizations such as the National School Boards Association and the American Association of School Administrators.

The American Council on Education has always endorsed unreservedly the granting of funds to accredited colleges irrespective of their church-relatedness. The American Civil Liberties Union has insisted that a college comply with the following three provisions before it becomes eligible for tax support:

1. Admit all students without respect to religion.
2. Require no course in theology nor attendance at a religious practice.

3. Place the control of the college in the hands of academic and not ecclesiastical officials.

The Horace Mann League, the plaintiffs in the Maryland college case, proposed a set of six norms by which the eligibility of a church-related college for tax support should be judged. These six norms are far more sweeping than the provisions urged by the ACLU. Indeed they constitute a revolutionary departure from every previous norm suggested as a "litmus paper" to test the "church-relatedness" of an institution.

The six norms urged by the plaintiffs in the Maryland college case have no basis in the *Everson* decision, in the Sunday law rulings or in any other federal or state judicial decision. Since the six norms were adopted by the majority of the Court of Appeals of Maryland it is important to record them as they were enunciated in the opinion of Chief Justice Prescott:

"(1) the stated purposes of the college;

(2) the college personnel, which include the governing board, the administrative officers, the faculty, and the student body (with considerable stress being laid on the substantiality of religious control over the governing board as a criterion of whether a college is sectarian);

(3) the college's relationship with religious organizations and groups, which relationship includes the extent of ownership, financial assistance, the college's memberships and affiliations, religious purposes, and miscellaneous aspects of the college's relationship with its sponsoring church;

(4) the place of religion in the college's program, which includes the extent of religious manifestation in the physical surroundings, the character and extent of religious observance sponsored or encouraged by the college, the required participation for any or all students, the extent to which the college sponsors or encourages religious activity of sects dif-

ferent from that of the college's own church and
the place of religion in the curriculum and in extra-
curricular programs;

(5) the result or 'outcome' of the college program, such
as accreditation and the nature and character of the
activities of the alumni;

(6) the work and image of the college in the community."

Having adopted these six norms, the majority of the Maryland court applied them to the four defendant colleges and
ruled that only Hood College could escape the constitutional
ban on aid to those institutions which the court, again bor-
rowing from the plaintiffs' brief, stigmatized as "sectarian
institutions."

The Maryland court sought to justify its conclusions by
reference to the norm enunciated by the United States Supreme Court in the Sunday law cases—the purpose and/or
primary result test. The Maryland court, however, became
involved in a basic contradiction since it explicitly conceded
that the "purpose" of the challenged grants was a public and
secular one but that the "primary effect" of these grants
was to aid religion. It seems difficult to conceive how a grant
of money intended for a public and secular purpose can be
so transformed that its "*primary* effect" is to aid religion.
It is clear that a *secondary* effect could be the aiding of
religion but the United States Supreme Court which furnished this test specifically ruled out aid only if the "*primary*" effect is the advancement or the inhibition of religion.

The three judges who dissented in the *Horace Mann* case
made the points that one would expect. But the overall
quality of the dissent was generally disappointing. It may be
significant to note that one of the judges on Maryland's
highest court, disqualified from participating in the *Horace
Mann* case because of a connection with one of the colleges
involved, in a subsequent opinion rejected the basic rationale
of the majority of the court that decided the *Horace Mann*
case. It is not impossible therefore that the Maryland court

on a future occasion could reverse its doctrinaire ruling in the *Horace Mann* case.

It seems safe to predict that scholars and experts in constitutional law will generally be unable to accept the reasoning and the result of the *Horace Mann* decision. Professor Paul Kauper of the University of Michigan Law School, a Church-State expert and an official of the Lutheran Church, expressed his disagreement with the Maryland decision in the *Alabama Law Review* (Vol. 19, p. 275) as follows: "Certainly it cannot be said that anything actually held in the United States Supreme Court's decisions to date requires this result." Professor Kauper goes further and asserts that:

> "It seems quite clear to me that the Maryland court disregarded the reasoning of the *Schempp* (the Bible-reading) case when it held that the First Amendment required the state to discriminate on the basis of the religious factor against certain colleges that satisfied the state's secular purposes."

Professor Kauper adds that in his judgment the Maryland court converted the establishment clause into "a sword of discrimination" and that such a construction "cannot be reconciled with the concept of neutrality" which is so prominent in Supreme Court decisions.

This judgment of Professor Kauper is similar to a viewpoint expressed in a student note in 1965 in the *Harvard Law Review* where, in a passage cited by the dissent in the *Horace Mann* decision, the author, after pointing out that some 800 of the 2,000 institutions of higher learning in America are church-related, writes as follows:

> To exclude these 800 institutions of higher learning from federal aid would seriously hamper the effort to increase enrollment capacity to the point where colleges will be able to handle the expected demand of 1970. . . .
> Such pragmatic considerations would be irrelevant if the command of the Constitution were clear; the remedy would then be a constitutional amendment. However, the lack of an effective alternative should be highly

relevant when a plausible constitutional defense can be made and where, in an area of Church-State overlap, criteria can be formulated which minimize governmental intrusion into religious concerns without paralyzing governmental attempts to cope with urgent national problems.

The key concept in evaluating the problems involved in governmental programs to aid private colleges is probably the definition one attributes to the terms "public" and "secular." The government may clearly finance only those programs which are public in the sense that they contribute to the common or public good. In general all such public programs would also be secular in view of the fact that the state may not directly aid the sacred or the sectarian. But if it eventuates that a tax-supported program achieves not only the secular end for which it was established but also advances religion, does the Constitution stipulate that such an arrangement is permissible only if the state could not reasonably attain its legitimate secular ends by means which do not aid religion?

Existing law contains no entirely satisfactory answer to that question beyond the *"primary* effect" test noted above. And this test breaks down the moment one tries to discover the real meaning and outside limits of the term "secular." The Maryland decision tends to define "secular" as "non-religious" or even "anti-religious"; the Maryland decision in effect means that the state may subsidize only that type of learning which is communicated devoid of any pro-religious or anti-religious orientation. The Maryland court held in substance that any college which seeks to have its students understand the secular more fully by giving to these students simultaneous instruction in the sacred thereby forfeits its right to public support. The premise behind such a conclusion is the assumption that education itself is *per se* secular and that therefore its administration belongs to the state. Consequently those whose minds tell them that an exclusive concentration on the secular by a college will result in a distorted sense of the secular must operate colleges pursuant to this conviction without state funds.

The concept of "no-aid-to-religion" can, as is thus seen, lead to the unconscious suppression of pluralism and to a state-imposed cultural monism. The monopoly on tax support of the public school at the elementary and secondary level has tended to promote this result although any meaningful discussion of alleged cultural monism in the public school is usually halted abruptly by the claim that public schools of less than collegiate rank *should* promote unity and inculcate democratic ideals. Few would proclaim that the promotion of national unity or the advancement of democratic ideals are duties of colleges, but at the same time the voices pleading for a deliberate governmental policy of fostering cultural pluralism at the college level are not very strong or clear. The pressures inherent in American society to homogenize all opposing ideas and to inhibit nonorthodox persons and groups will be intensified and will lead to the most serious distortions if a simplistic principle of "no-aid-to-religion" is applied as the *one* controlling principle to determine the government's policy with respect to aid for church-related colleges and universities.

The Maryland decision means that the government may give support for concededly secular purposes *only* to those colleges which have expressly adopted a policy of isolating secular learning from all considerations of sacred and sectarian learning. The basic fallacy—indeed the unconstitutionality—of such a conclusion is the undeniable preference it gives to one philosophy of education and to one view of human existence. The Maryland opinion, to put it another way, places the vast prestige and taxing power of the state on the side of those institutions of higher learning which have openly declared that they will impart an education in secular subjects with the explicit understanding that these subjects can and should be learned without reference to any Scriptural, sacred or even spiritual realities with which they may be intertwined.

It may be objected that the Maryland decision does not actually go that far. Such an objection has some validity but it must be remembered that the eventual thrust of the rationale of the Maryland decision would be the withdrawal of every bit of governmental support now available to church-related colleges, even perhaps to the scholarships and loans for which students at these colleges are now eligible. If, furthermore, substantial governmental assistance is essential for the very survival of private colleges, then church-related colleges, under the Maryland decision, would be living on borrowed time.

The intention here is not to exaggerate the importance of the Maryland college decision. In order to place it in perspective it might be well to sum up the dangers in the opinion as well as the reasons why the Maryland decision may be only a lonely happenstance in American jurisprudence and not a landmark ruling likely to establish a trend.

Some of the dangers inherent in the Maryland opinion are the following:

1. Many Americans tend to have an excessive reverence for any view which a court states to be the law. Consequently the impact of the Maryland decision on legislators, educators, and public opinion molders could be great. This impact is heightened by the fact that the decision was allowed to stand unreviewed by the United States Supreme Court.

2. The Maryland decision offers a plausible and easy to comprehend interpretation of Church-State separation. The decision's flat "no-aid-to-religion" theory is appealing and cogent. Its credibility is increased by the fact that it was not applied indiscriminately but selectively to only three of the four colleges involved.

3. The decision's ban on aid to a Protestant college will in all probability increase its plausibility. Catholics and others who might suspect anti-Catholicism as a motive if only Catholic colleges had been barred from tax support cannot make out a case on this ground since Western Maryland, a Methodist college, was put in the same legal category as the

two Catholic colleges.

Some of the reasons which suggest that the Maryland decision may not have a powerful or lasting influence are the following:

1. The 4 to 3 ruling is overwhelmingly against the prevailing viewpoint among college and university educators. The American Council on Education, the most prestigious and influential voice of higher education in America, committed itself to file a brief *amicus curiae* urging a reversal of the Maryland decision in the event the U. S. Supreme Court agreed to review it. The position of the A.C.E. continues to be one which endorses aid for *all* accredited colleges.

2. The Maryland decision is at sharp variance with the formula used in all federal legislation designed to aid higher education. The Maryland opinion moreover appears to be more rigid than the stated position of the American Civil Liberties Union and even of Protestants and Other Americans United (POAU).

3. The tenuous coalition which made up the majority of the Maryland court, the weakness of the arguments of this group of four judges and the emerging criticism of the *Horace Mann* decision by legal scholars may well be factors which will cause the gradual withering away of whatever impact the Maryland decision may have had.

Whatever the *Horace Mann* decision may eventually come to signify, there are lessons in it for Catholics and for everyone interested in the future of church-related colleges in America. Some of those lessons will be clear from the conclusions and recommendations which follow.

IV. CONCLUSIONS AND RECOMMENDATIONS

It would be most encouraging if anyone were able to set forth a master plan of strategy and tactics by which the private colleges of America could reverse the forces which are now threatening the possible annihilation of these institutions. These forces are, of course, not primarily legal or constitutional but flow from the massive secularization of American education and of Western culture. The law and judicial decisions interpreting the First Amendment tend inevitably to reflect and to institutionalize that secularization. It is doubtful whether even our written Constitution with its twin guarantees concerning religion and the state can prevent the law from becoming another instrumentality of a secularized society.

Law, on the other hand, educates; law forms and fashions public opinion in ways which sociologists have hardly ever explored. It is important therefore that everyone concerned with the future of church-related colleges work to minimize the impact of those forces which brought about the unprecedented and revolutionary Maryland decision.

1. CATHOLIC INVOLVEMENT IN CHURCH-STATE LITIGATION

The conclusions noted above lead to a recommendation which is placed first because it must be considered before any other approach or strategy can be sensibly undertaken. This recommendation urges that if Catholics and others who believe in the unique value of private colleges are to prevail in having their viewpoint accepted, they must not allow themselves to become involved in the wrong lawsuit at the wrong time and on the wrong issue.

All of these "wrongs" converged in the Maryland case. It was the wrong lawsuit because the Catholic colleges were not only clearly on the defensive but were clearly more "sectarian" than the two other defendants. It was the wrong time because the Maryland Court of Appeals had two other Church-State cases pending on its docket; these cases involved tax-exemption of church property and state aid to church-related hospitals, both of which were resolved on behalf of the religious groups involved. It was the wrong issue because the defendant colleges were forced to litigate on the assumption that an accredited liberal arts college can somehow be transformed into a "sectarian" institution.

Catholics in American history have generally allowed themselves to be sued rather than to sue with respect to their rights in education. The one brilliant exception was the litigation initiated by the Society of Sisters and a non-denominational military academy in 1923 protesting the referendum in Oregon which would have outlawed all private schools. The unanimous ruling of the United States Supreme Court in the famous *Pierce* decision of 1925 vindicating the right of private and parochial schools to exist is evidence of the usually valid proposition that in America those who seek to broaden constitutional privileges by affirmative measures and aggressive litigation generally prevail.

The *Everson* case is to some extent an example of Catholics allowing themselves to become involved in litigation at the wrong time and on the wrong issues. In the 30 or more Church-State cases pending in late 1967 Catholic organizations were, in the vast majority of instances, defendants in a suit brought by a coalition of strict separationist groups, whose lawyers have generally found or fashioned a fact situation which is generally very favorable to the plaintiffs.

None of the pending Church-State lawsuits involves tax support for denominational colleges. But the decisions in current cases involving the Elementary and Secondary Education Act (ESEA) and grants from the Office of Economic Opportunity (OEO) will almost certainly affect the results of those court rulings about aid to church-related colleges which inevitably must come.

Consequently Catholics should be involved as much as possible in each of these lawsuits. Involvement by official spokesmen for the Church is not, however, always wise or appropriate. It is significant to note that the National Catholic Welfare Conference filed a brief *amicus curiae* only once in American history, in the *Everson* case in the United States Supreme Court. Participation by Catholic groups of citizens and parents can be very effective, especially if it is clearly spontaneous and not "arranged."

Catholics must face the fact that they are in confrontation

with a very powerful campaign of judicial "lobbying." This campaign is directed by an informal coalition of groups united by a desire and determination to have American constitutional law state that all aid to church-related schools violates the establishment clause.

This campaign is not entirely new but its momentum has clearly increased with the enactment of the ESEA in 1965 and the continuing use by OEO of church-affiliated agencies. The legal talent available to the groups sponsoring this campaign is very impressive and is likely to win important victories. The legal talent on the defense side is, with some exceptions, composed of attorneys for dioceses and/or assistant attorneys general or assistant U. S. attorneys, few of whom have had substantial experience in litigation with respect to Church-State matters.

It seems clear that the Catholic laity and even Catholic jurists have little idea of the importance of pending Church-State litigation. This profound ignorance derives in part from failure on the part of Church officials to reveal how much each school or diocese receives and is likely to receive from ESEA, OEO and other programs. Full disclosure by Catholic educational authorities plus lay and parental participation in decision-making are two developments which are indispensable prerequisites to involvement by Catholics in the crucially important court cases now being processed. If this involvement came about it might develop into a situation where Catholics would be plaintiffs and not defendants, attackers rather than the attacked, shapers of issues rather than defenders of laws.

2. CATHOLICS AND COLLABORATION AT THE STATE AND REGIONAL LEVEL

Clerical control of Catholic colleges has been one of the many reasons for the failure of Catholic institutions to take the initiative with respect to state and regional plans and legislation designed to strengthen private colleges. To be sure *all* state and federal plans to assist private colleges are very recent. But if Catholic colleges continue to fail in supplying the leadership and initiative needed to inaugurate programs to extend to private colleges some parity with their public counterparts, these programs may simply never come to be.

In some states Catholic colleges clearly constitute a balance of power which, in an alliance with Protestant and private colleges, could blunt the movement towards a monopoly on higher education by the officials of the public university establishment. Action by Catholic clerics, however, is likely to be misunderstood. But the combined efforts of the faculties of Catholic colleges in proposing a state plan for the advancement of private colleges might have an amazing impact.

These efforts, however, probably cannot be successful, or even initiated, without a board of trustees made up of a broadly-based group of community leaders. If a board of trustees, all known leaders, speaks for a private college of which they are the real governing body, their voice is far more likely to be heard than the voice of a lay or clerical faculty group from this college urging governmental action to insure the survival of private colleges.

The creation, therefore, of real decision-making boards of trustees for Catholic colleges is not only desirable but probably absolutely necessary if Catholic and other private colleges are to organize themselves and present a successful plea to legislatures and to the court of public opinion on behalf of private colleges. Catholics furthermore should remember that colleges affiliated with the Catholic Church in America constitute some 40 percent of all the church-related colleges in the nation. The inactivity of Catholic colleges or their inability to act with respect to state aid to private institutions of higher education may therefore be such a significant factor that state plans to aid *all* colleges cannot develop without Catholic initiative.

Leadership by Catholic colleges, always in cooperation with private colleges and, whenever feasible, with state-related universities, should seek to stress the implications of freedom of choice in selecting one's college and the desirability of maximizing this freedom by extending financial parity to all private and public colleges and universities. The freedom of choice principle is presumably adhered to generally, but the number of high school seniors who enjoy any meaningful freedom in selecting the private college of their choice is declining sharply every year. If Catholics believe that this freedom of choice is a precious privilege they should organize and act to preserve it, independently of the presence or absence of advantages for Catholic institutions. Catholic educators, in other words, must take their stand and state their reasoned position on the virtues and values of private higher education. It is fair to say that no Catholic group has yet done this, with the result that the credibility of Catholic educators is sharply decreased since it is assumed that Catholic support for programs to give governmental aid for private colleges is motivated largely if not exclusively by self-interest.

The support which Catholic educators should lend to the enactment and implementation of laws to aid private colleges should not derogate from Catholic moral support for public colleges and universities. Here again Catholics face a credibility gap. Has any group of Catholics ever recognized and praised the purposes and principles of a system of state-related technical schools, colleges and universities? It seems true that Catholic educators have grudgingly admired the state university whose growth they cannot deter but have never really joined wholeheartedly in movements to expand the services of state-related higher education.

The involvement of Catholics and Catholic college officials therefore in state or regional plans to benefit private colleges must first overcome the passive resistance to these efforts which may arise because of the public's presumption of self-interest on the part of Catholics and from the past silence by Catholic educators about the needs and values of state-related higher education.

Despite all the built-in difficulties, however, Catholic college officials in many states are the only ones who can launch a state plan for private higher education. It is probably not an exaggeration to predict that unless officials of Catholic colleges exercise at the state level a good deal of leadership in the very near future, virtually all private colleges could decline dramatically and even collapse.

If Catholic educators are to extol the values of the private college and advocate for it a position of partnership or parity with public colleges, Catholics must face up to the fact that the private college is deemed to be highly desirable because it believes in and possesses academic excellence. This critical issue brings us to our third point: Catholic colleges and academic excellence.

3. CATHOLIC COLLEGES AND ACADEMIC EXCELLENCE

A booklet summary of the 1965 Danforth study on church-related higher education in America entitled *Eight Hundred Colleges Face the Future* concludes that the group of 817 colleges surveyed contain "*some* of the finest colleges in America, but also *many* of the poorest" (emphasis as in the Danforth report). Over 20 percent of the 817 are not accredited, while "at least one third of the whole group is marginal." Another third "lies in the broad middle range of quality," while the "last third compares favorably with the best public and independent institutions."

Although the Danforth study does not so state, Catholic colleges fall roughly into these three categories. The rapid improvement of marginal Catholic colleges may be not only desirable in itself but may in fact be absolutely necessary if these Catholic colleges are to receive significant government grants. This necessity comes from the fact that governmental programs for higher education are and will continue to be geared to provide incentive matching grants for colleges seeking to conduct experimental programs or to provide partial funding for buildings to accommodate an

expanding enrollment. Colleges which are marginal will probably be unable to demonstrate the minimum self-generating initiative required to obtain matching funds from governmental, or foundation, sources.

The phasing-out of marginal Catholic colleges should therefore be considered with the utmost seriousness by the highest possible officials. The very suggestion of the phasing out or the consolidation of some Catholic colleges brings one into direct confrontation with the almost chaotic diffusion of responsibility in America for the inauguration and maintenance of Catholic colleges. The problem is not unique with Catholics. The Danforth report states the point this way:

> No one can justify the operation of four Presbyterian colleges in Iowa, three Methodist colleges in Indiana, five United Presbyterian institutions in Missouri, nine Methodist colleges in North Carolina (including two brand new ones), and three Roman Catholic colleges for women in the city of Milwaukee.

The same report goes on to say that the problem of the "unplanned establishment of colleges" is "perhaps more acute in Roman Catholic higher education where the various religious orders and congregations are free to begin new colleges without any central restraint, and bishops often encourage the founding of institutions for which they have no financial responsibility."

A "paper" solution for this problem is easily imagined—a central national authority in the United States which must give its approval prior to the establishment of any new Catholic colleges. The Church clearly possesses the power to conduct such a supervisory agency, as the Holy See does with respect to assignments to religious groups in the foreign missions.

The key to the effectiveness of the Holy See in carrying out the deployment of personnel in foreign missions is, of course, the money dispensed by the Vatican to authorized missionary groups. In the United States no such "power of the purse" exists with respect to Catholic colleges. It may be that the creation of a national endowment fund for Catholic higher education is a necessary prerequisite to the control of the unplanned proliferation of Catholic colleges.

It should be noted that the emphasis placed on episcopal collegiality by Vatican II should operate not merely to give to bishops, acting together as a national or regional unit, more autonomy from Rome. Collegiality should mean that individual bishops should not act unilaterally in important matters—such as establishing a new college—without prior consultation and approval from their brother bishops within the same nation or region.

The problem of the proliferation of Catholic colleges and the unsound expansion of existing Catholic colleges into universities is surely one of the most crucial issues in Catholic higher education today. A part of this problem comes from the fact that a large number of Catholic colleges for women have been established in this century—in an era when, since 1900, virtually no other liberal arts colleges exclusively for women have been founded! If co-educational colleges are required, both because of public opinion and possibly because of sound Catholic theological principles, some radical transformations will have to occur at Catholic colleges for women in America!

Resistance to the expansion of Catholic higher education can be anticipated on the familiar if sometimes unspoken premise that at least at Catholic colleges young Catholics will "keep the faith." The assumption here, of course, is that a widespread defection from the Church occurs among Catholics who matriculate at non-Catholic or state-related colleges. Even granting the validity of this assumption (for which there appear to be no valid statistics), the implications of the attitude that at Catholic colleges at least students "keep the faith" need exploration. This attitude, which seems to be pervasively widespread in the Catholic community, suggests the following observations:

The viewpoint that the primary purpose of a Catholic college is to preserve the faith of its students was the foundation of the successful case of the plaintiffs in the Maryland college litigation. By employing pious "rhetoric" found in the catalogues and literature of the two Catholic colleges involved, the plaintiffs fashioned a powerful argument to the effect that the principal and primary purpose of the Catholic colleges was the indoctrination of students in Catholic philosophy and theology.

No one, of course, is suggesting that Catholic colleges compromise their purpose in order to acquire state funds. Every college, moreover, is expected to offer some type of character formation and moral guidance. But is it not time to state clearly and unequivocally that the *primary* purpose of a Catholic college is to give an education in the liberal arts and in secular subjects?

Such a statement does *not* mean that the religious function of a Catholic college is "secondary" but rather that the courses about religion and theology available at a Catholic college are an integral part of the total education imparted. The inculcation of piety and similar pastoral objectives will thus be viewed not as a part of the academic program of the college. Whatever piety or spiritual formation may be hoped for from a Catholic college should not be the anticipated result of academic or scholastic training.

Some may feel that such an emphasis on the sacred sciences *as sciences* is exaggerated. Granting that the terms "primary" and "secondary" as applied to the purposes of a Catholic college can be misleading, it is insisted here that Catholic colleges are not compromising their principles but rather clarifying them when they assert that their primary and principal purpose is to impart an education in the arts and the sciences *as such*—to Catholics, non-Catholics and non-Christians.

If this primary and principal purpose is confused or clouded by some vague apostolic or pious intention, there is no little danger that the basic academic integrity of the institution can be harmed. Putting it another way, one can say categorically that unless Catholic colleges seek first and foremost academic excellence for its own sake, they are likely to be neither good colleges nor effective as institutions designed to "keep the faith" of their patrons.

If Catholic leaders commenced their thinking and planning with regard to Catholic higher education with an uncompromising and undeviating determination to start and perpetuate Catholic colleges only if they are and can continue to be academically superior, dramatic changes would be required. Countless good effects would flow from the drastic and dramatic results which would follow honest and rigorous application of the principle that the Church cannot tolerate Catholic colleges unless they are academically superior. One of the not inconsequential results would be the fact that such academically superior colleges would be invulnerable to an allegation, advanced in a lawsuit or before a legislative body, that they are merely "sectarian" institutions whose primary mission and purpose is to preserve the religious faith of those who attend them.

SUMMARY

The legal and constitutional status of Catholic colleges is not an easy question to resolve at this particular time when both the law and the meaning of Catholic higher education are in a state of rapid transition. Resourcefulness, vigilance and careful planning are qualities which are indispensably necessary if Catholic and other church-related colleges and universities are to survive.

Federal legislation will probably continue to be favorable to *all* private colleges but state programs must be accelerated. Methods of neutralizing the impact of judicial "lobbying" must also be developed.

The first and foremost objective which Catholic higher education must endorse and attain is true academic excellence. Regardless of any and all consequences, academic superiority must be established as the only goal worthy of a Catholic college which seeks as its prime objective the development of the rational powers of man.

The future status and even the very existence of private and church-related colleges in America are by no means certain. It may be that Catholics, sooner than we may imagine, will be required to face the fact that public opinion and the law will not sanction governmental assistance to church-affiliated colleges. But until or unless that time arrives, the Church in all of its agencies and with all of its energies should dedicate itself anew to the beauty of all secular learning and to the transcendent importance of rational men creating and transmitting new knowledge.

BIBLIOGRAPHY

The following is a list of a few important recent books on higher education. A list of all books or articles of a significant nature about Catholic higher education will be found in the extensive bibliographies contained in the first two volumes noted below.

CHURCH-SPONSORED HIGHER EDUCATION IN THE UNITED STATES, Report of the Danforth Commission, by Manning M. Pattillo, Jr. and Donald M. Mackenzie. American Council on Education, Washington, D.C., 1966. 309 pages, $6.00.

This study is without doubt the most comprehensive survey ever made of the 817 church-related institutions of higher learning in the United States. It contains a wealth of new information about denominational colleges, a series of reasoned and balanced recommendations and a 16-page bibliography of books and articles on higher education in America. This book will be the definitive study in this area for the foreseeable future.

THE SHAPE OF CATHOLIC HIGHER EDUCATION, Edited by Robert Hassenger. University of Chicago Press, 1967. 378 pages, $8.95.

This collection of 11 essays focuses on several contemporary problems facing Catholic colleges in 1967. Some of the papers tend to be too technically sociological to be meaningful to all persons involved or interested in the future of Catholic higher education. The book, however, contains many valuable items, not the least of which is a 20-page bibliography.

THE CONTEMPORARY UNIVERSITY, Robert S. Minson (ed.). Beacon, 1967. 364 pages, $2.45.

This excellent collection of 15 essays by outstanding educators is a republication, with significant additions, of the Fall, 1964 issue of *Daedalus*, the Journal of the American Academy of Arts and Sciences. It is a volume which is virtually essential to anyone associated with higher education.

STAFFING AMERICAN COLLEGES AND UNIVERSITIES by James F. Rogers, U.S. Office of Education, 1967. 220 pages. 65 cents from U.S. Government Printing Office.

This study surveys the needs of 1,809 institutions of higher education for professional personnel in the period through October, 1969. It contains an extraordinary amount of information and data, all indicating that the task of recruiting college professional personnel will continue to become ever more urgently necessary.

**FINANCING HIGHER EDUCATION, 1960-1970, Ed. by
Dexter M. Keezer. McGraw-Hill, 1959. 304 pages, $3.50.**
Although this study containing 12 separate essays was issued
before the revolutions in every aspect of higher education which
occurred during the 1960's, it remains nonetheless one of the most
valuable over-all surveys of the nation's economic potential in rela-
tion to the needs of higher education.

Designed, produced and distributed by Geo. A. Pflaum, Publisher, Inc.

General Editor: Russell Shaw, Director of Editorial Services, National Catholic Educational Association

NCEA Papers: *No. 1 The Parish School Board by Rev. Olin J. Murdick*

No. 2 Team Teaching: A Rationale, by Melvin P. Heller, D.Ed.

No. 3 The Purpose of Catholic Schooling, by James Michael Lee

No. 4 Catholic Adult Education, by Vaile J. Scott

No. 5 The Constitution, Governmental Aid and Catholic Higher Education, by Rev. Robert F. Drinan, S. J.

Subscriptions to NCEA Papers (five titles, bimonthly, September through May) are obtainable at $7.50 per subscription. Copies of individual titles are available at $1.50 per copy. Discounts on quantity orders of individual titles are: 10 percent on 7-13 copies; 20 percent on 14 or more copies. On orders of less than $5.00 not accompanied by payment, a 45-cent postage-handling charge will be added. Make checks payable to:

National Catholic Educational Association
NCEA Papers, Box 667, Dayton, Ohio 45401